500 Positive Affirmations for Abundance Money and Wealth

Powerful Affirmations to Reprogram Your Mind for Success (Law of Attraction)

By Creed McGregor

Disclaimer

The information provided in this book is meant to provide helpful information on the subjects discussed. The publisher and author are not responsible for any health needs that may require medical supervision and are not liable for any damages or negative consequences from any treatment, action, application or preparation to any person reading or following the information provided in this book. References are provided for informational purposes only and do not constitute endorsement of any websites or other sources.

Copyright© 2016 Maddog Publications All rights reserved. No part of this publication may be reproduced, distributed, or transmitted in any form or by any means including photocopying, recording, or other electronic or mechanical methods without prior written permission of the publisher and author. Except in the case of brief quotations embodied in critical reviews and certain other non-commercial uses permitted by copyright law.

While attempts have been made to verify that the information contained in this book is accurate, neither the publisher nor author assumes any responsibility for errors, omissions, interpretations, or usage of the subject matters herein.

This publication contains the opinions and ideas of its author and is intended for informational purposes only. The publisher nor author shall in no event be held liable for any loss or other damages incurred from the usage of this publication.

Introduction

The word affirmation means to provide emotional support or encouragement. When we affirm something to ourselves we are convincing our minds to believe that what we are affirming is true. This can be a two edged sword. Our mind will believe a negative affirmation just as much as a positive one. Unfortunately, in the world we live in today most of what we hear and tend to believe is negative. We constantly affirm negative thoughts to our subconscious mind without even realizing it.

This is why doing the opposite, by purposely channeling positive thought to our minds, can have such a wonderful effect. Positive affirmations can change your life. Have you ever been broke? How about unhappy in a relationship? Perhaps you've failed at something that you set out to achieve. Don't worry because we all have. Think about your mindset you had during those times. It's likely that you were broke, unhappy, and set up to fail because of your negative thoughts, or lack of positive ones.

If you fear being broke or say things like, "I never have enough money" or "I can't afford that" then you're right. Henry Ford said, "Whether you believe you can do a thing or not, you are right." This is the two edged sword. Although you never wanted to be broke, your fear and negative thoughts about it actually made you broke. The same goes for relationships, careers, health and so on.

"All that we are is the result of what we have thought. The mind is everything. What we think, we become." *Gautama Buddha*

In order to reprogram your subconscious mind to achieve success you simply have to change your thoughts. This can be easier said than done. We have between 50,000-70,000 thoughts per day or 35-48 thoughts per minute. It's quite a task to monitor all that gear spinning 24/7. But we can gain control of our thoughts and crank up the positive vibes with a little practice.

There is no doubt negative thoughts will try to creep in every now and then but learning to recognize them is the key. When you are consciously aware of your negative thoughts you can stop them before they do damage. When you catch yourself saying or thinking a negative thought grab ahold of it and give it a good dose of positive thinking.

For example you may say, "I can't afford that." This is negative even if it's true. If you always affirm to yourself that you *can't* afford something then you never *will* afford it. Instead, stop that thought and say, "How can I afford that?" This gets your mind thinking of ways to achieve it. To help you recognize when you're being negative, familiarize yourself with the words can't, don't, haven't, not, won't, and shouldn't.

When you recite positive affirmations, be very clear about what you want and always affirm in the first person and present tense. For example don't say, "I'm becoming wealthy" but rather, "I am wealthy." If you say you're *becoming* wealthy, you're telling your mind that you are *someday* going to be wealthy but that day isn't today. This thinking is always in the future and never in the present. It will always be in the future, meaning it will never become reality.

When you read affirmations, be sure to do so with feeling. Your feelings and emotions are what bring you closer to realizing your goals. Your thoughts, negative or positive send out a frequency or vibration that bring more things like it into your life. That's why when you're having a pity party or feeling depressed, everything seems to go wrong. The same is true when things are going good.

All too often, though, we sabotage our good thoughts and before we know it things get bad again. Maybe you think when things are good, things are too good or maybe that you don't deserve good things and then all of a sudden you're right. Stop those thoughts and your life will change drastically for the better.

Send out vibrations of positive thoughts and you'll be amazed. Read as many positive affirmations as you can daily. It's best to read them first thing in the morning to set your mood for the day. Read them again at night before falling asleep. Read them anytime throughout the day if you notice negative thoughts trying to creep in.

Some affirmations may seem a little quirky or even comical but laughter and amusement are positive emotions and part of the overall recipe of success. As long as you're sending out positive vibrations about abundance, money, and wealth your life will change for the better.

500 Powerful Affirmations for Abundance, Money, and Wealth

Money comes to me easily.

I can afford anything I want.

I create money and wealth for myself.

My wealth is limitless.

Abundance is all around me.

My eyes are open to the vast abundance.

I am deserving of wealth and abundance.

I open doors in my life for money to flow into.

Money is good and can be used for good.

Money makes me a better person.

Money is a tool I can use to help others and myself.

Everywhere I look is opportunity.

Wealth and abundance are commonplace in my life.

I am currently wealthy.

I make money with ease.

I am a money magnet.

Money is energy and I open my arms to it.

Money allows me to give more.

I have many revenue sources.

New money is being printed right now and will find its way to me.

There is more than enough money to pay my bills.

I have money to pay my bills off early.
I receive more money everyday.

Money is attracted to me through positive thought.

Money has no choice but to flow my way.

I invest my money in smart ways.

My money helps to create more money.

I deserve the wealth and abundance I'm experiencing.

My income is constantly increasing.

Success and wealth are attracted to me.

I send out positive thoughts that bring me more success.

Money comes to me from all directions.

Money loves me and I love money.

There is more than enough money to keep me rich.

I love being successful and happy.

I am able to buy things I need without worry.

I have no fears about money.

Money is my friend and we are inseparable.

I live on the fast track of making money.

I build assets with my money.

I have no emotional barriers in regard to money.

The past is the past and today I am rich.

Money does not care where I came from.

I'm in complete control of my finances.

I understand the purpose of money and I respect it.

My wealth is not limited to any set amount.

I love the feeling of being rich.

I choose abundance today and everyday.

Abundance is overflowing in my life today.

I am able to manifest more wealth whenever I need it.

Creating wealth is effortless to me.

The more money I make the more I can share.

My attitude towards money is continuously positive.

I close my eyes and see wealth all around me.

I'm so grateful for all the riches in my life.

If I want something I buy it.

If someone I love wants something I buy it for him or her.

I find new ways to create wealth everyday.

I'm so wealthy it's ridiculous.

I do so much good with my money.

I create opportunities for others with my money.

The more I give the more I receive.

The seed of money making is rooted in me forever.

I really do have a tree that money grows on.

My positive attitude keeps my abundance limitless.

Money is a tool I use for good and to help others.

I am just as deserving as anyone to be rich.

I choose to accept the energy source of money into my life.

I buy myself things because I want to and because I can.

I am financially free.

I hear abundance knocking so I let it in.

My life without abundance is not even possible.

I love the smell of money.

I am so happy with my abundant life.

I feel lucky but I know I deserve abundance.

Being wealthy is fun and exciting.

Wealth shows me the way.

Money follows me wherever I go.

I feel so blessed that I'm wealthy.

I bathe in wealth and cleanse my spirit.

I'm doing more good in the world now that I'm wealthy.

Abundance is everywhere I look.

I make more and more money every month.

I have a surplus of money and wealth.

Money is good to me and I am good to money.

I am rich, I am wealthy, and I am successful.

Success to me is like breathing; I don't even have to think about it.

Every deal I make is successful.

Opportunity finds me.

I'm open to all money making opportunities.

Money can't resist gravitating to me.

Great abundance is what I deserve.

I'm abundant in every aspect of my life.

I can make money in my sleep.

My dreams at night are of wealth and abundance.

I wake up each day to new opportunities.

I hear of opportunities and I take advantage of them.

I have wealthy friends and relationships.

Success comes easily to me.

Successful ideas come to me all the time.

Money making ideas fill my mind.

No money making deal escapes me.

I'm in tune with the song of money.

Green is my favorite color.

My bank account increases with little effort.

The bank calls me for a loan.

I'm able to make deals without fear of failure.

I invest my money in ways that make it grow.

I'm a magnet for success and wealth.

I create opportunity through positive thoughts.

I am rich because it is my right.

I accept wealth as part of who I am.

I could not stop my abundance if I tried.

Nobody can discourage my wealth attracting abilities.

I get busy living because it's what I deserve.

I am a money making machine.

Wealth flows to me like a downhill river.

I open my arms and accept wealth into my life.

I feel the energy of wealth radiate around my body.

If I jumped off a cliff so would money.

Wealth and me go hand in hand.

My wealth is so abundant it spills onto others.

I love the riches that I experience.

I love being wealthy and rich.

Feeling wealthy and abundant is feeling alive.

To me abundance is easy.

Every breath I take draws more money to me.

Money finds its way to me no matter what.

I am the path that money chooses.

I reprogram my mind to achieve success.

My subconscious mind is full of positive thoughts.

My mind is sending out positive frequencies that attract abundance.

My wealth is meant to be.

The power of my thoughts attract money.

Wealth appeals to my thoughts.

Abundance for me is inevitable.

I am who I am and I am wealthy.

I have all I need and then some.

All my needs are taken care of.

I am happy with where I am today.

Riches give me opportunities to be a good person.

I will leave a legacy of wealth when my time comes.

I love life and the abundance it shares with me.

I'm grateful for wealth and cherish the things it provides me.

I will not forget where I came from and will share my wealth.

I see visions of more abundance heading my way.

I do not fear wealth or abundance.

I feel comfortable around money and wealth.

I am secure financially.

I understand the power of wealth and control it well.

I am a master of wealth.

Having plenty of money is my human right.

I trust that money and wealth are not evil and are used for good.

The more I spend the more comes back to me.

I enjoy spending money on people I love.

I have an unlimited supply of money to share.

My birthright is to be abundant.

I have my piece of the pie and then some.

Money finds me when I least expect it.

I imagine money warming me like the sun warms my body.

I make room in my life for more money.

I make financial goals and fulfill them easily.

I value my success.

I have the golden touch when it comes to money.

I am lucky when it comes to money.

I am grateful for my prosperity.

I am as rich as I want to be.

I earn an enormous amount of money.

The universe delivers money to me.

For every dollar I spend two come back.

I give myself permission to embrace wealth.

I am a millionaire in many ways.

I am focused on my success.

I've achieved more wealth than I can imagine.

My success has made me very generous.

I give myself permission to accept more money.

I fear nothing about money.

Money enters and exits my life freely as needed.

I understand the function of money and admire it.

I'm in awe of all my wealth and abundance.

Others ask me for advise in regard to money.

My money investing skills are top notch.

I invest in ways that return money ten fold.

I'm tuned into the frequency of wealth.

All I do is emit positive vibrations that return abundance.

The force of abundance is with me.

I think positively therefore I am abundant.

My life is everything I dreamed it would be.

I love helping others and giving unselfishly.

I have complete faith in my money making skills.

I am rich and wealthy in so many ways.

My cheerfulness and excitement create so much wealth.

My inner spirit is focused on creating abundance for all.

I love who I am and that wealth makes me a better person.

I give back to my community in many ways.

I cherish all my wealthy and abundant friends.

My inner child is living out my wildest dreams.

My focus on creating wealth is laser like.

I cannot be derailed from the successful track I'm on.

No one's criticism can weaken my strong will to be wealthy.

I do not hear others skepticism, it falls on deaf ears.

I'm more determined than ever to keep my abundance.

My abundance is far more than just money and wealth.

I am more positive that ever at every aspect of my life.

I conquer the game of wealth.

I stand atop the tallest mountain and open my arms to abundance.

Abundance strikes me and charges my spirit like a bolt of lightning.

I'm glowing with riches and everyone sees it.

My abundant spirit ignites a fire in me and those around me.

I am one with wealth.

The power of positive thought creates anything I want or need.

My many investments bring me more money.

I build my own infrastructures to create wealth.

I'm financially free of liabilities.

My mind's positive charge fills me with riches.

I am wealthy today because I choose to be.

I continually find ways to increase my income.

People trust my judgment in regard to wealth creation.

I was born to create wealth and abundance.

Being wealthy is my destiny.

My life's fulfillment is to express my love through wealth.

Wealth is a positive and substantial tool I use for good things.

My wealth creates wealth for those around me.

I am wealthier than any king in history.

My riches open the floodgates of creativity and prosperity.

Mountainous piles of money await my commands.

When I close my eyes I see myself floating on clouds of money.

I connect with the energy source of money and use it to charge my spirit.

I'm an abundant human being living out my fantasy.

I take vacations to wherever I desire.

I buy luxury items because I can.

I go places and meet people most only dream of.

Others speak of my wealth as well earned and deserved.

I give more than I receive whenever I can.

I have no fears of losing wealth.

I can gain more wealth and abundance with a snap of my fingers.

I'm a whirlwind of abundance.

I leave a path of wealth creation for others to follow.

I create so much wealth it seems magical.

The universe is my genie and I have unlimited wishes.

Money rains from the sky whenever I want it to.

I'm a wealth of good fortune.

Generating money is second nature to me.

The world is full of opportunity and my mind is open to it.

I hone in on opportunities like a hound dog.

I take advantage of good deals and multiply my money.

I use money to make more money in endless amounts.

My money stretches to infinity and beyond.

Anyone could have the wealth I do if they only knew.

My success in controlling my thoughts makes me rich.

I think, I focus and I win every time.

Money to me is a tool to be the best person humanly possible.

Wealth helps me express my love to the world.

I am richer each day with each new opportunity.

Each day to me is another opportunity to increase my abundance.

I'm grateful for all my abundance and to be more alive than ever.

I help those in need in many different ways.

Money allows me the freedom to be what I'm supposed to be.

I create passive income so I don't have to be a wage slave.

I'm resistant to negative people and thoughts.

My thoughts remain positive throughout the day.

The secret to my success is all in my mind control.

I'm the driver in control of my greatest asset; my mind.

I think wealth and I become wealthy.

I'm grateful to have learned the secret to wealth.

Controlling my thoughts has a direct impact on my wallet.

No one is smarter or more creative than me; we are all equal.

Wealth making opportunities are available to us all.

I grab what I can from the opportunities presented to me.

I want to be rich therefore I am rich.

Thinking in a certain way has made me a wealthy person.

My mind is under my control and I steer it towards abundance.

When I think wealth, I have no choice but to be wealthy.

My riches come to me directly through my channel of thought.

To be wealthy is merely my thought process.

I chew up negative thoughts and spit them out.

Negative frequencies sound like static to me.

My mind is set only to the channel of positive thought.

When I think abundance, it has no choice but to honor me.

I don't speak negativity because I don't want to think it.

My mind has been cleansed of any negative thoughts or emotions.

Wealth comes when I'm positive, which is everyday.

I create wealth from what some would consider thin air.

Wealth comes to me because I call for it.

I whistle for wealth through my thoughts and it comes running.

Some consider me lucky but it's really my thought process.

I generate wealth and abundance like it's going out of style.

I have more money than I have ever had.

I am a millionaire of abundance.

Wealth, success, abundance and riches are all I think about.

My abundance is not just measured in money.

I have an abundance of support and love.

My relationships are rich with joy and companionship.

I have a wealth of friends and family that admire me.

I reach out to those in need and it brings me joy.

My riches increase whenever I am unselfish.

With each seed I plant another money tree grows.

I fertilize my seeds of money with positive thought.

Through purposeful thinking I am wealthy.

My life is abundant in all areas that exist.

I enjoy the challenges of each day and welcome opportunity.

I make a dollar for every positive thought and that keeps me going.

At 50,000 thoughts a day there is unlimited wealth opportunity.

When others are down I lift them up.

I share my wealth by having no fear of losing it.

I admire money and the purpose it serves.

I respectfully decline to think anything other than abundance.

Life is to be enjoyed and I am doing just that.

I trade money for services I need whenever I need them.

Money buys things that make me happy.

Money does buy happiness when I stay positive.

I visit places around the world I've always wanted to see.

Money allows me to enjoy many things.

If opportunity was a tree then money does grow on trees.

I can see a wealth opportunity from a mile away.

Loads of money are yet to come my way.

I create wealth by thinking it to death.

My focus on every money goal I set is precise.

My path to wealth is clear cut.

I sneak up on a wealth opportunity like a ninja.

My clear thinking makes it easy to make money.

Since cleaning up my thinking, I have become rich.

Money finds it way to me with little effort.

I am more alive today due to my overwhelming abundance.

I teach others what I have learned and they too become wealthy.

I do not dream about owning things, if I want them I buy them.

I am a billionaire when it comes to wealth.

I own several vacation homes.

I vacation overlooking the ocean.

I visit overseas because I can.

Traveling is easy for me because I am rich.

I can afford to visit anywhere I want.

I can afford to send my family and friends on vacations.

I don't win by chance; I win buy unanimous decision.

I'm living the life everyone was meant to live.

I am richer than I once thought possible.

To be rich is my spiritual right.

I have lots of money but I'm rich in so many other ways.

Wealth starts from within so I focus on that.

We all dream of being rich, I dream of being richer.

The wealthier I become the more I shine.

I find strange and new ways to make money.

I make money at things I've never imagined.

Money is so abundant everyone could be rich if they really wanted to be.

I am claiming my piece of the rich pie.

I have every right to be as rich as I want.

Creating money is not a problem for me.

Finding ways to create wealth is fun for me.

Wealth generating is a game that I'm undefeated at.

Deals find me when I'm not even looking.

I can spot a good deal and know just how to act on it.

The more money I set free the more comes back to me.

Life is easy when I have this much money.

My savings account is the largest account at the bank.

I have money hidden everywhere.

I have multiple savings accounts because it's too much for one bank.

I can live off the interest my money earns.

I play the stock market like a fiddle.

I invest in slightly riskier investments that pay off huge.

I own lots of real estate that grows in value.

I own businesses that make lots of money.

I own assets that increase my net worth.

I give to charities frequently.

I host charity events that raise lots of money and awareness.

I create foundations that help those in need.

My passive income is much larger than my liabilities and expenses.

My wealth creates more wealth and keeps multiplying.

My wealth will make my children and grand children rich.

My wealth will last for generations to come.

My riches will give future generations many opportunities.

I will be remembered as giving and unselfish.

I will be used as an example of how to become wealthy.

I will live a long and prosperous life.

I celebrate everyday like it's my first and last.

I do what I can today to help others be wealthy.

I give to those that deserve better opportunities.

I don't blame circumstance.

I get up and create the circumstances I want.

My challenging past has no bearing on how I finish.

My wealth allows me to think of new ways to inspire people.

Wealth shines on me like the sun on a warm day.

I believe in opportunity for everyone.

My thoughts today are a flowing river of positivity.

My generosity is long reaching.

I'm grateful life pushed me around in the past to shape who I am today.

My wealth creates a domino effect of generosity.

I help others become better people.

Love is abundant is my life and I'm grateful for it.

For me, believing is how I create my reality.

I think and grow rich.

For I am everything I can be at this moment.

I treat others how I like to be treated.

I respect others with the same respect I deserve.

Money frees me from the hassles of life.

Money releases me from the shackles of the rat race.

I can express myself more with the freedom of wealth.

I can do things I've always wanted to do.

I can try new things because of my wealth.

I can be creative in new and amazing ways.

Being wealthy has allowed me to quit my dead end job.

My family is happier because of the wealth I've created.

I am healthier because of my wealth.

I have more time for exercise.

Money allows me to focus on my health and myself.

I can afford to eat healthy food.

I no longer have to eat cheap unhealthy food that makes me sick.

Wealth has given me new life and hope.

I share my hope and dreams with others to inspire them.

I can buy the car I've always wanted with all the bells and whistles.

I can afford to go to the movies whenever I want.

I can afford to eat at fancy restaurants and invite the whole family.

I can afford to pick up the tab when at lunch with friends.

I can afford to walk into a bar and buy a round of drinks for everyone.

I can afford to go to sporting events and pay for expensive box seats.

I can afford to help others do things on their bucket list.

I can afford to do everything on my bucket list.

I can afford to go to any music concert I want to.

I can afford to go to plays and musicals.

When on vacations, I can afford to indulge as much as I want.

I can afford to deep sea fish if I choose to.

I can afford my own fishing boat.

I can afford a speedboat for recreation.

I can afford to scuba dive in beautiful waters.

I can afford to go on a cruise.

I can afford to throw huge parties with expensive food and cocktails.

I can afford the most expensive bottle of wine.

I can afford the most expensive steak dinner.

I can afford to pay off my house.

I can afford to keep my family safe and secure.

Money is my ticket to the life I've always wanted.

I make money with so much ease it seems effortless.

I keep my ears and eyes open for money ideas and opportunities.

Friends and family let me know when there is a deal I might be interested in.

I can afford to take risks to gain big rewards.

Playing the stock market is fun for me.

I have enough money that risking some is no big deal.

I invest in real estate deals that grow my money ten fold.

I buy land because it's a good investment.

I purchase property for recreational use.

I buy homes and rent them out for passive income.

Money is the tool I use to be a fruitful and giving person.

Everywhere I look I see fresh opportunities.

Money cannot elude me.

Wealth and abundance are brimful in my life.

Wealth, abundance, and riches describe my life.

I make money no matter what I do.

I make money with no exceptions.

I love what I do for a living and money is only a side effect.

Investing and growing my wealth is a hobby for me.

I am good at avoiding bad deals.

I only get into good investments.

I rely on my intuition when it comes to money.

My instincts in dealing with money are impeccable.

My thoughts are so positive, that negativity has no chance.

My force field against negativity is always on.

I avoid negative people and circumstances.

I sidestep bad deals with crafty precision.

My money only goes into things that make it grow.

Wealth has given me a new perspective on life.

The past is irrelevant and does not shape my future.

I have turned things around in my life.

I have gone from being broke to being rich seemingly overnight.

I changed my thoughts and the world around me changed.

My perception of the world is so clear now.

Life seems so much easier now that my thinking is on track.

I'm free with my money buy not careless.

I respect the old mighty dollar and praise it's existence.

Without money the world could not function efficiently.

I have no more fear of real money than people do with play money.

Money does not make me feel nervous.

Money does not create anxiety in me.

Money does not rule me; I rule money.

I am the master of money and it works for me.

I don't work hard for money.

My money works hard for me.

I have the mentality of a wealthy person.

My mentality is that of the richest people in the world.

Very wealthy people think differently than most and I see that now.

I practice thinking and acting like the richest people in the world.

I meditate about wealth and bring it into my life.

My focus on wealth goals is a laser beam that cannot be broken

I create opportunity that positively affects many others.

I touch the hearts of others through unselfish giving.

I build abundance in everything I do.

I tell others about the secret of positive thinking.

I share the secret of positive affirmations with everyone I know.

I share how I built my success.

I brainstorm with others on creative ways to help others.

There is no lack of abundance in my life and never will be again.

I read positive affirmations daily so I can keep all I have gained.

Speaking affirmations aloud helps me feel them more.

I write some of my own affirmations for fun.

I stopped watching the news because it's so negative.

I only read and pay attention to positive events.

I am inspired by rich people and mimic their habits.

I have several rich friends that mentor me often.

Nothing matters to me more than sharing my abundance.

I read affirmations on other topics besides wealth and money.

All aspects of my life are important to me.

These are my thoughts and beliefs about money, wealth and abundance.

The End.

Printed in Great Britain
by Amazon